MW00928542

# North Flame

*A fable with pictures for all ages*

by Rufus Goodwin

Illustrated by Lisa Schofield

Copyright © 1999 Educare Press

FIRST EDITION

Published by Educare Press
PO Box 17222
Seattle, WA 98107

International Standard Book Number: 0-944638-16-3

Library of Congress Cataloging Card Number: 99-67038

Printed in China

10 9 8 7 6 5 4 3 2 1

Design by Megan Haas

# North Flame

Contents:

I

Not long ago Betmar lived in the City of Gray Towers. Betmar loved mornings, when the day broke, and the soft evenings too when lights went on, windows lit up, and the whole City shone in darkness.

Winter went hard that year. One evening, great flakes of ice fell just as the lights turned on. The town soon glittered. Betmar gazed out her window as whiteness blurred the Gray Towers. Thick quilts of snow drew quickly over the pavements.

Night deepened, and Betmar fell asleep dreaming

of snow. As dawn neared, the air turned colder. In the furnaces of the City even the fires began to freeze. One by one lights went out, broken by ice. The river East and the River West hardened and thickened. No more water ran from the faucets. Drifts blocked the doors. Ice pasted shut the windows.

So cold did it get that the City slowly froze and stopped. No more sun shone through. Dark and still, the City lay buried.

Betmar tiptoed into her parent's room. Stretched in the dark, there they lay, both asleep like ice. Betmar listened, and waited –nothing moved. She called. No one answered.

She went to the window. Opening it, snow fell into the room, and Betmar fell out. She landed in a bed of white winter.

The houses and streets looked like glass. The City towers rose like icicles. Betmar sat up and called again –no one came. Nothing in the streets moved.

II

Alone in the frozen street, Betmar began to cry. Her tears froze like pearls, then fell one by one into her cupped hands. A black crow flew by pinching a silver coin in its beak.

The glint of tears caught the crow's beady eye. It cawed, flapped its wings, and landed on Betmar's foot.

"What's all this?" the crow asked, dropping the coin into her shoe.
"The City is frozen," Betmar said.

"True, but who cares?" the crow returned. "If it bothers you, go North and fetch the fire. Ice will melt from the towers like tears. Water will reflow in the River East and in the River West. Cross over the Great Bridge into the country. Keep going until you come no further. There you will find a path to the fire."

The crow crooked a wing. "I just gave you good advice. I must feed my fledglings. What have you in return?

Betmar could only shrug.

"You shall give me your tears," the crow demanded. Greedily, he pecked the tears from her cupped hands until he had swallowed them all.

"Travel light and keep out of sight." So saying, the crow again cawed and flew off.

Betmar rose. The bird vanished. Betmar plodded after, putting down foot after foot until she reached the bridge that loomed ahead like a dream rising into the clouds. Across the bridge she walked on into the fields. Even the treetops had been buried by snow. Her feet sank deeper and deeper, and she stumbled to her knees. Not far off a light shone, but her heavy eyes shut.

III

Betmar woke under warm covers on a cot against the wall. Her room was plain. A pale light shone through the window and she heard feet shuffling in the hall. A large, round woman came in.

"I am the farmer's wife," she told Betmar. "I've brought you some soup."

"It's well it was cold and we needed wood," the woman added. "My husband found you half frozen in the snow. Now keep under the covers. Tomorrow is another day."

The farmer's wife tucked the covers tight, smiled, and left. Betmar stared at the ceiling wondering which way was North. Soon she dozed.

Next morning she woke bright and lively. The

farmer's wife served breakfast and set her to work. Betmar collected eggs, swept, and washed up. Around the farm the hilly pastures rolled like waves into the distance. Betmar, by the time Spring came, felt quite at home.

In the vegetable patch one day when she was alone and it was warm, a busy brown worm working in the earth spoke to Betmar. "Snow and rain have come and gone," said the worm. "The earth is soft. Have you forgotten the great ice in the City of Towers?"

"No," said Betmar.

"The countryside is lovely," went on the worm, "But no fire burns in the clay."

Afterwards, Betmar dreamt of the frozen City. In her dream she met a large rabbit who wore a patch on one eye. He was gnawing trees. At breakfast next morning, Betmar told the farmer's wife that the time had come to leave. The good round woman grew alarmed. "You have been most kind," Betmar said.

Tears came to the farmer's wife's eyes as out of her shoe Betmar took the crow's silver coin and laid it on the table.

The farmer came in just then and overheard. For a time he looked sternly at Betmar. At last he lowered his head and said quietly to his wife. "Summer is coming."

That night the three of them ate cozily in the kitchen. The farmer's wife packed a picnic basket, and they laughed at how Betmar first came into the house like a frozen log from the woodpile.

IV

At dawn, Betmar trudged off. From the farm into the forest was a short way, but the further Betmar went, the thicker the woods grew. There was no telling one side of the trees from another. She was soon lost and began to cry.

This woke the rabbit that had been snoozing inside a nearby tree. The rabbit opened his one eye, saw Betmar, and bounded out so quickly that he terrified her.

Quite so," cried the rabbit as he saw Betmar jump. "What's in the basket?"

"Eggs," said Betmar. "I'm headed North."

"So," said the rabbit. "In that case, hand me the basket. Why are you headed North?"

"To fetch the fire," Betmar told him.

"It's a long journey," the rabbit sighed, taking her basket. "You should go home instead. Where do you come from?"

"The City of Gray Towers," said Betmar.

"I see. In that case," the rabbit added, "you are here now. Every tree has many sides. Keep walking away from the side you are on. That is the path."

Then the rabbit scolded her. "What will you eat tomorrow? People go South without provision, but nobody goes North without food."

With some dismay, Betmar watched the rabbit eat her picnic.

The rabbit snorted. "Instead of crying so much, consider me. One eye! You should give me one of yours. Yes, an eye!"

Betmar took fright at this. "Here," said the rabbit impatiently. He snapped his fingers in her face. "There... I have it!"

He laughed and rubbed a finger against his thumb. "It shan't get lost. Look!" The rabbit wiggled a floppy ear, stuck a finger in it, and swallowed. "There," he cried. "Now your eye is in my ear. Remember that!"

"How can that be?" Betmar asked in surprise.

"Because," said the rabbit. "I know where I hide my Easter eggs. Look here!"

Betmar stuck her head into the rabbit's hole in the hollow tree. Inside it was just like Easter, full of carrots, eggs, and marzipan. But when she pulled her head out, the rabbit, picnic basket, and even the hollow tree were all gone.

V

That night Betmar found another hollow tree. She ate nuts and slept peacefully. Next morning she walked on.

On the third day it grew dark. Soon she walked in woods where no sky lit the ground. The shadows thickened. So thick grew the forest that she no longer knew night from day. At last, Betmar saw only a dull blackness.

She moved darkly from tree to tree. She put her arms around the trunks. She pressed her hands over the bark. Her travel took time. Betmar sometimes forgot where she herself stood. She certainly would have given up except that in front of her two bright eyes turned on, glowing like small lamps. The glowing eyes blinked. "Welcome to the dark," a deep voice said. "I am the owl. I know all about the darkness, so ask me a question."

"Oh gladly," said Betmar. "How can I find my way here without light?"

"No light?" the owl hooted. "That's a happy one. And where are you headed?"

"To fetch the fire," said Betmar.

"Oh no! Oh my! A solemn matter," said the owl. "But the light! A hoot for light! Who needs light?"

Betmar said she did.

"And what for?" asked the owl, most interested.

"To see," said Betmar.

"Trees need light," cried the owl. "But you found my eyes in the dark. Now how is that?"

Betmar kept silent.

"In the dark," the owl went on, "the light is inside. In my eyes you saw the inside of the darkness."

The owl hooted several times.

"If I were you, little friend, I'd forget the fire. Listen instead. Listen much harder! If you can't see, maybe you can hear. A quiet bird knows when to fly. He who listens hears which way to go."

With another hoot and then a screech loud enough to wake the trees, the owl's eyes shut.

VI


Betmar stood steeped in the silence of the forest. She hoped in vain that the owl's eyes would open again. She listened. At first she heard the loneliness. Slowly the sound of breathing trees reached her. But the darkness was all that stared back at her. Then she began to walk. The footfall of her own feet reassured her.

Soon she heard the great hush of all things. This hush sounded like a hymn growing louder, of rocks, of earth, of stones, of trees.

The Hush, the great silence, swelled out of the humming quiet, and with these mute words, like an owl singing:

Deep in the dominant deed
Flows the dark on like a river
Till the burnt day done runs down,
And sky-drowned, its water fall free.
Then shall the sleeping stones wake
Rolling heavenwards to high stars;
Glow shall the dark lowly worm
As earth renews the old bones.
Over the dark rushing of river
True shall the tree bend shining
Branch to the child of cold current
Who climbs clay to the upward shore.
Down shall the fruit of raw season
Fall like a hail harvest of seed
And Woe's to woman shall rise bravely
From brittle death of pale battle.
Bright shall the wind blow strongly
Our starred gray skulls to the sun;
Half cracked shall a crooked moon melt
And each enter arms of its kind…

A hollow silence, ominous, swallowed the hymn.
As from the throat of a dark angel, Betmar heard
her name followed by the silver thread of a song:

Go gently maid...

Light flashed in the sky. Betmar gazed up. A treetop
burst into leaf. A singing star had opened.

Be not afraid.
Your breath, your mouth
Are North, are South.

Unutterably tired, Betmar tumbled into a cold sleep.

VII

Pale yellow light, when she woke, filled the cold sky. She lay alongside a rocky field that stretched as far as the eye. Blown and blasted brown grass and the gray bush of winter grew flat. At her back the forest fell away. On the edge of the tundra, every path led off alike.

She would again have cried, but a large gray elephant wandered by, greeted her politely, and confessed – with much irritation – to being lost.

"I would never be here," the elephant added, "except that my friends in the jungle gave some very poor directions. Parakeets and Chimpanzees do chatter. Crows too. My advice to a girl like you is be careful what you listen to. You might get lost in the tundra and wake up one day in the jungle. Too much tongue wags the tail, as the baobab says."

Betmar felt pity for the great beast and patted its thick, gray hide. "As for me, out of the woods, without any trees," Betmar said, "the space is so light and flat that if I move, I may go in all directions at once."

"Just go back where you came from, which is best, I assure you," the elephant told her. "I wish I could. There are at least ashes in the old hearth, as the baobab says. I have been to the North Pole inside a whale. Believe you me, it was no fun. Nothing but ice."

The Gray City of Towers, Betmar told him then, was frozen too. She was on her way North to fetch the flame. The elephant had been to the pole. Surely he had touched the flame?

"Not on your life," answered the elephant. "I am

no friend of flame. I love the deep dull vapor of mud and broad leaves heavy in puddles. The tundra is all desert. No fronds fall, the baobab says, from a chopped forest."

"Go through the spaces between the trees," Betmar suggested, "and watch out you don't bump."

"Good," said the elephant. "I hope your friends give better advice than mine."

The elephant uncurled its trunk towards Betmar and dumped some peanuts into her lap. "The only trouble with peanuts," said the elephant, "is shucking the shell."

"As the baobab says," added Betmar.

The great beast fixed one tiny eye on Betmar. "If you want truly to travel North," it told her, "look above the tundra tonight for a star the size of my eye and white as my tusk. I wish I could give you a ruby in heaven. But the star will have to do. I'll be watching. As the baobab says; it's better to have a companion even when travelling alone."

## VIII

Across the tundra, the days grew longer, nights shorter. Betmar slept mornings. Evenings she walked toward the star. It shone, as she had been told, like the elephant's eye. At night, she heard wolves.

The flatness of the tundra tired her. Soon in the moonlit monotony she forgot where she was and why she had come. Overhead it clouded. A skudding sky hit the stars. The shadowless flatness stretched before her, and she sank down on a glacial stone, looked at the ground, and suddenly longed to be back in the City of Gray Towers. A wolf howled, this time nearer.

When Betmar looked up, wolves crouched in a circle around her rock, baying at the sky. They filled the night with howls, yet she was not afraid. The wolves gave Betmar a certain frightening pleasure.

Like cries from a dungeon, the howls echoed into the distance and into the night. Only the leader of the pack pawed his way forward until, in front of her rock, he bowed slightly. Eyes as sharp as teeth took her in, and the wolf's jaw wagged.

Betmar believed, as any girl might, that the wolf had come to eat her, and her alone. Where on the tundra were others like herself, other girls who had left the Gray Towers behind?

The wolf growled. It growled, however, quite politely and correctly. Betmar somehow understood. The pack of wolves wanted not food – they wanted for Betmar to dance!

To dance! Even as she thought this thought, the

whole pack howled. Their wolf chorus rose like a gale in the night, and Betmar heard the beat of her own heart. The pack leader's paw led her into the circle of the wolves. To their wild howls, she moved slowly – then faster, till like a dervish darling, Betmar spun dizzily.

Overhead the sky whirled. Betmar saw the wolf's eyes fastened on her. Behind its high head the tundra whipped like a flying cloud. Her feet beat faster to the howling and the padding paws until the horizon blurred. The wolf's teeth twinkled like stars, and Betmar spun off – as a bird across the wilderness.

## IX

A windy sea beat at Betmar's feet the next morning. The gray and blue waters were flecked with ice. She saw no boats. Only the high shadow of the North hung in the sky. The ocean reached lonelier ahead even than the vast tundra. Betmar shook and shivered.

How could a girl fetch the fire with no boat; how could she follow the star further?

She pictured the Gray Towers of her old home, the country side, the forest and the tundra. The crow had said to go until she could go no longer.

Now, before her, the cold depths ran silent under the wind. No Gray Towers, no farm, no forest, no crow, no farmer's wife, no worm, no great rabbit, no owl, and no elephant. Only the sea. Sea, and a dark slippery rock asleep by the shore.

As Betmar splashed new tears on the back of the rock, the rock shivered. It rose, twitched, and then stared at Betmar out of two deep brown, still sleepy eyes.

Betmar let out a silent yelp!

It yelped back!

Before her, an old wrinkled seal smoothed its whiskers. Then it asked Betmar, "are you the butcher from the backland come to spill my blood and take my pelt to the stainless factories?"

The seal squinted at her. "No. I see you are a child. What brings a girl to the tundra, to the edge of the wind iced with salt?"

Before Betmar answered, the seal nodded knowingly, as if all things were understood. Then it said: "But it is not time to fetch the fire."

A voice from behind them suddenly replied: "Time may be against us, but not against you!"

The old seal peered about. Only the tundra stretched behind them. "Whose voice is that with you, child?" the seal asked suspiciously. "Or are you a false one?"

"The great rabbit," answered Betmar.

"What, may I ask, can a rabbit know of the water?"

"He sees us out of the elephant's eye," Betmar answered.

"That is so," added the Great Rabbit, "and out on the sea there floats an island of ice. Old seal, if you swim there with Betmar, you shall have the food of the Gods."

Then the great rabbit was gone.

X

With Betmar riding on his back, the old seal swam off.  Betmar's bones soon ached.  The sleeker and slicker the seal swam, higher and higher rose the waves.  Sea spray knifed her face.  The churning white and blue laughter of the waves now howled.  Under them, the deep shadow of the ocean gathered like night.  Far off, through the singing salt spray, the iceberg seemed to move towards the horizon.

As on a rocking horse racing against a dark night, Betmar crested from wave to wave.  The sky above hung like heaven's hour of death.  Fatigue stormed down over Betmar.  She forgot the iceberg.  She saw no more.  A stupor engulfed her.

On the face of this deep darkness she dreamt that a

light shone, and that music played a sound of the sea. The wind sang. High above, the sky fluted. Out of the deep, from beyond the horizon of her dream, slowly the City of Gray Towers rose, and its cryptic spires sparkled.

Ice no longer clung to the gray glass. High up, windows opened. Black and white birds flew into the dusk.

A swelling flock gathered on the fleeting layers of the sunset. Light dipped beyond the edge of the world.

The birds, like the last rays of the sun's glory, also flew from sight.

Then Betmar spoke a prayer of the night. She spoke it to the ocean. Her words fell like rain onto the waves.

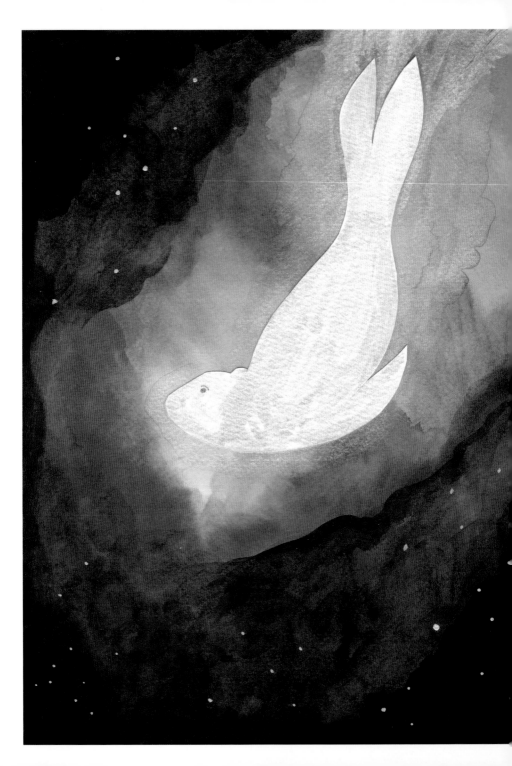

XI

Betmar woke upon a shelf of silver ice. Still cold, still ominous, the sea washed at her feet. At her back rose a shadowy wall of jagged snow.

The seal dozed all day. Betmar watched the cloudy sky blow overhead. The wind tattered the ocean's waves. Evening approached and it grew chilly, the sky cleared, and the seal woke.

"Tonight it comes," the seal told her with finality. "You shall sail the iceberg alone." The seal rose on its flippers and sniffed the raw sea air. "The fish are deep," it said, "the mouth of the ocean is shut. The wind chases itself. The night is dark. The stars shine fragile."

"Besides," the seal added with a sneeze, "I have caught cold. I'm exhausted."

The seal read Betmar's thoughts and went on: "If you want to thank me when you return to the City of Gray Towers, raise a statue – in dark stone – of a seal watching the sky."

Its eyes met Betmar's. "My head is empty from swimming," the seal said. "But the stars are full. When we fail the stars, stars bend to us. Each star has its fate. Each star has its task. We seals are the stars of the arctic. In the polar sea we swim like lights live in the dark sky."

"Now," added the seal, "I advise you. The iceberg floats on further. Watch carefully, be thankful, and remember. The Great Rabbit, the eye of the elephant and we seals brought you so far. We timed your travel. As memories grow old, you may think of and thank us. How? That, friend, is always the great secret. Like stars, we are memories' messengers. You may also be one. Night helps all stars to shine. Even when gone, we seals may still help you. You who live may help us. Darkness helps the light."

High in the sky, while the seal said these things, a star fell. It was the star that, above the forest, had opened and sung. Betmar noticed the slow fracture of the light, yet without alarm, lulled by the sea and the seal's words, she watched the falling star. It quickened. The spark streaked across the night growing lighter.

"I see," said the seal calmly, as Betmar pointed.

It now dazzled like a diamond split in a light beam. It flashed nearer. Behind the peaked cap of the iceberg, the darkness drew back into the distance. The streaking star alone seemed to fill the sky, like a burst seed.

The seal watched. "Betmar," it said quietly, "The secret of the sea is to love. Death is a miracle."

The seal leaned forward. Its soft whiskered nose pointed alive into the sky. Like a lion, then as Betmar watched, the seal sprang into the air and was gone.

She blinked. In a moment her eyes again saw the streaking star near at hand overhead, and the seal was flying through the sky with open jaws. In a jolt, the star had died out. Incandescent, the seal now shone transparent and brilliant. Betmar momentarily stood blinded.

A shadow of light, dark as steel, was all that remained where the seal and the star met, and the seal with the brown eyes swallowed the star.

## XII

Betmar fainted. She lay in a cold sleep on the ice. A fog curled by, hovered over the water, wrapped in the ice, and the night settled down. As the sea churned, the iceberg moved North. From the sky, a far off music shimmered like falling curtains.

Betmar dreamed again, now of lying locked in a house of ice. Frozen columns barred her entrance and exit. Halls of snow led one into another. The ceiling and floors glistened, hard and polished. Nothing stirred. Nothing breathed. She dreamt of burning thirst in this crystal room, unable to move.

The saying goes that unless it spouts even a whale can hide in the ocean; but once it spouts, the harpooners shoot.

On her bed of ice, Betmar floated across the great polar sea. She slept as unseen as any whale far beyond the sights of people in the City of Towers.

But if you could be in heaven and look out, you would have seen Betmar upon a boat of beauty. You would have seen her stretched on a mirror of ice, reflected in the snowy sea. Her eyes shut, her face intent on a dream.

If you saw her, your heart would fill. Such would be the mirror's distant untouchable coldness that you would long for tears, like liquid laughter, to cool and moisten the dry desserts and dusty streets.

The Great Rabbit had said, "It is sometimes a long time before a short time passes."

Betmar, in her dream, did not hear the Great Rabbit splash up, his long soaked ears flopping heavily in the salt waves.  Part dark, part light, the sky hung over the water as the Great Rabbit swam pushing the iceberg along, and talked.

"Soon your eyes will open, Betmar," said the rabbit, "and again you will see a different world.  So it should always be with sleeping and waking.  Your trip has brought you a long way.  You may yet travel further.  It is not always easy to say.  The sea teaches us to look sometimes, sometimes to reach out – and sometimes to shut like the shells.  Every sea drinks from another ocean.  When great waves wash the world away, be wise.  Be calm."

Betmar stirred. The rabbit whispered: "It may be easy. It may be hard. Your sisters may never cross a country, a forest, a tundra, climb an iceberg, and catch a falling star. Keep warm. Stay well. Beware of ashes. Every fire throws ashes except one. Seek that, and you will find all."

From a corner of the dawn, over the sea, the sun flashed warm and bright against the ice. Betmar woke. The Great Rabbit, heading on to the House of Wheels where he lived and was again due to inspect the gyrations, ducked under the sea.

Betmar rose.

She stood and gazed at the sun. There was the City of Gray Towers, with the snow melting, the icicles dripping.

In a secret and invisible way, hope is not just a face on sadness – but hope is true and real. Betmar stood by herself at the window. Ahead of her stretched a journey, just as if the City of Gray Towers, the country, the forest, the tundra, and the ocean lay behind her. She thought of the old black crow who had drunk her tears.

For a moment, no ashes fell in her heart. She urged herself to keep on, to catch that star. She vowed to try to remember, and to tell this tale.